AF375427

No Pain No Gain

The Gift of the Credential of Pain

Loran Joly

ReEnvision Press

Contents

Chapter 1
NO PAIN, NO GAIN?

Some people say that Pain is a GIFT.

Or, that WITHOUT PAIN, there is NO GAIN.

Or, that PAIN is a CATALYST for massive GROWTH.

***

Yet others say we need to FAIL, and FAIL, A LOT.

And by FAILING, they are referring to a process of EXPERIMENTING, actually.

***

So, might we talk of a DIFFERENCE, between mere EXPERIMENTING, to gain knowledge ("failing"), vs knowledge gained from MASSIVE PAIN-inducement – which we would also typically call a FORM of FAILING, too?

Chapter 2

The Issue of Almost NOONE OPTING for MASSIVE PAIN as TRAINING

Because Pain-Training Has No Guaranteed Outcome

How many people OPT to go into TRAINING, in something arguably "painful", IF it has no STATISTICALLY-HIGH TRACK RECORD of PROVIDING GREAT RETURNS, a great RETURN on INVESTMENT, you might say?

For don't some of us say, that it is FOOLHEARTY to take a RISK of INVESTING MASSIVE TIME, MONEY, or PAIN, in something with a VERY UNPREDICTABLE OUTCOME?

***

But even MORE than the outcome being simply VERY UNPREDICTABLE, it also perhaps not offering a GREAT PAYOFF?

***

So, for instance, we might say that it is PAINFUL, in a way, to spend massive amounts of time and money, in a LONG-TERM SCHOOL PROGRAM.

Or, too, to spend massive amounts of PHYSICAL Discomfort, in going into a NAVY SEAL TRAINING PROGRAM.

Or, to spend massive amounts of time in MEDICAL SCHOOL, say.

***

HOWEVER, isn't the ROI – the RETURN on INVESTMENT of Medical School, say - rather STATISTICALLY PROVEN to COME OUT a certain way, IF we FOL-LOW the RECIPE?

IF we thus DO the WORK, that is? If we "LEARN" what the PROGRAM SAYS to LEARN? And if we are doing it EFFICIENTLY?   And if we of course COMPLETE IT, so that we have a TANGIBLE RECORD that we *COMPLETED* the TRAINING?

Chapter 3
A look at CREDENTIALS gives us IDEAS on ASSETS

Perhaps we might benefit by looking at how we size up our sources of information, guidance, leadership, or what have you.

For in my view right now, I see credentials as SHORTHAND to lend a quick SUMMARY of someone's supposed TALENT in an area.

For instance:

1. The Credentials that are based upon CLASSES one ATTENDS, in a Traditional (brick-and-mortar) "SCHOOL".

Or else...

2. The Credentials that are based upon CLASSES one ATTENDS, *OUTSIDE* of a Traditional (brick-and-mortar) "SCHOOL".

a. The "NON-BRICK" School of "BEING UNUSUALLY HIGHLY--LOVED".

b. The "NON-BRICK" School of "THE SCHOOL of PAIN".

(Otherwise perhaps called "The School of HARD KNOCKS").

Such as "prison" time, typically quite trauma-inducing, stigma-inducing, and more; or, if having dealt with a chronic, debilitating addiction; or a massive physical handicap, such as blindness, or massive deformities (see The Elephant Man), or even the loss of an eye (Peter Falk, of Columbo); or a severely crippling physically-maiming crime, such as what James Brady faced when shot in the head; or when forced to adopt a religion that turns out to be a cult; or when one loses a child, particularly if the child were in their twenties or thirties, say, and suddenly, too. Such as happened to Dominique Dunne and his daughter; or with the original host of Sixty Minutes, Mike Wallace; or anyone losing a child to a drug overdose. Or too, if *utterly "unfairly"* imprisoned for a long period of time, due to clear massive jurisprudence errors, such as happened to Anthony Ray Hinton.

Or if suffering a very life-threatening illness such as cancer, stroke, or a very debilitating heart attack.

c. The "NON-BRICK" School of "RELIGION".

d. The "NON-BRICK" School of OBSERVING.

e. The "NON-BRICK" School of THINKING – in other words, the School of US-ING LOGIC.

As per the book, then, "Think and Grow Rich".

f. The "NON-BRICK" School of USING a LOT of INTUITION, by which one's "thinking" is done while BYPASSING the USE of WORDS, words, especially, that are generally USED in BOOKS.

Hence the phrase, "A PICTURE Is WORTH a THOUSAND WORDS".

This NON-WORD-based "thinking" being urged by Buddhists, for instance, and some in the Mindfulness Meditation groups, where it is urged to "THINK LESS" – to think less with WORDS, in other words, and to THINK MORE, with anything BUT words, such as INTUITION, or VISUALS, such as PICTURES or PAINTINGS.

Hence, too, ART Therapy....

***

I reserve a SPECIAL CATEGORY for WORDS that are found and used ONLY in groups of people with little or no READING being done, and only VERBAL and thus, too, FACE-TO-FACE communications being done, as in some so-called "Primitive" societies, or areas which are often called "undeveloped".

(See the works of Hugh Brody, perhaps, who wrote, amongst his books, "The Other Side of Edasn: Hunger-Gatherers, Farmers, and the Shaping of the World", in which Chapter four is entitled "WORDS".

Chapter 4

PERHAPS the BIGGEST PAIN-Training-Centers Are From Those With Utterly SLIM TRACK RECORDS of SUCCESS?

We might consider, now, that the GREATEST _REWARDS_ may come from the GREATEST _RISKS_ TAKEN.

And one of the GREATEST RISKS one could TAKE, is one with a LONG SHOT PAYOUT?

In other words, the MORE RISK TAKEN, the more the POTENTIAL PAYOFF.

***

And what MAKES for a PAIN-based TRAINING options having a POOR OUTCOME, typically?

***

In my estimation, a CRITICAL factor in HOW Pain is PROCESSED, in CERTAIN kinds of Pain – the pains we REFER to as the "UNFAIR" – based Pains, is this, and precisely this, said as a chapter in and of itself, to follow:

Chapter 5

Pain-Training Apparently Has a Likelihood of BITTERNESS as a SIDE-EFFECT

Perhaps FEW come to PROCESS this pain, COGNITIVELY, in a way that does not result in BITTERNESS.

***

Chapter 6

MASSIVE Pain is Arguably CRUCIAL but not SUFFICIENT, for MAXIMAL GROWTH

C onsider this:

How many people do we know, who say,

"Life Dealt me a BAD HAND"?

Or,

"I got SCREWED"?

Or,

"I was NOT born with a SILVER SPOON in MY Mouth"?

Or, essentially,

"I'M a VICTIM" – whilst yet, a person who is not PHYSICALLY BRAIN-DAM-AGED, such that they literally CANNOT DO cognitive work.

***

Some would tend to refer to such, in perhaps somewhat derogatory words, as "Sore Losers", or "Whiners", or again, **BITTER.**

Or, "ANGRY" People.

Or, People who "CAN'T GET OVER it".

Or, People who "CAN'T FORGIVE".

.....

Chapter 7
Processing Pain Requires UNDERSTANDING the REASONS the PAIN-Source had COME to BE a "PAIN"!

It strikes me, from my own life, that it is far easier to understand, and then PROCESS, the PAINS that come from NON-People sources, than from PEOPLE.

So, it being easier to process the pains of CANCER, than a CLEARLY PEOPLE-based pain source.

***

And again, we would seem to find it VERY HARD to be BITTER, at CANCER cells, for their having IMPACTED us with massive pain.

Unless we were to turn angry at a DIETY – a GOD – for HAVING CAUSED this cancer.

But I don't think many go that route, or would find it even fruitful.

***

But when PAIN – and MASSIVE pain – is associated CLEARLY with a PERSON – or a GROUP of people – isn't it SO HARD to PROCESS this pain as ACCURATELY as NEEDED, so we are not BITTER, thus?

***

So we say, instead, "HOW '*UNFAIR*' this is".

But we NEVER say, "HOW UNFAIR of those CANCER CELLS to 'TREAT US so MEANLY, or that TORNADO, or that HURRICANE, ..."

Chapter 8
What We Need is MORE UNDERSTANDING of CAUSE AND EFFECT RELATIONSHIPS in PEOPLE

I attended some Alcoholics Anonymous meetings in the past year, out of curiosity, to see what was being said, and I learned a few fascinating things:

First, that the greatest gains in someone were tied to having come to conclude that they – and all people – DO the BEST THEY CAN, given WHAT they were HANDED, in their UPBRINGING, and their GENDER, and their RACE, and so on.

And too, as per what they are CURRENTLY being handed, in terms of the ENVIRONMENTS they are IN.

***

And SECONDLY, that there is a growing REALIZATION, in such persons, overall, that THERE IS A REASON for EVERYTHING.

And that, this could be called UNDERSTANDING: IF we have attained a great deal of skill at such.

***

And that one at least HAS come to say,

"I DON'T KNOW EVERYTHING".

and

"I'm perhaps WRONG about SOME things".

and

"IF ONLY I KNEW the WHOLE PICTURE, I would say, "WELL, OF COURSE they were the way they were...."

Chapter 9
What Makes UNDERSTANDING so HARD?

I believe that understanding PEOPLE has several factors that make UNDER-STANDING something that is VERY, VERY HARD to come by.

UNLIKE understanding SCIENTIFIC concepts, or how to GET to the MOON, or BUILD a COMPUTER, or FIX a CAR, or build an AIRPLANE, say.

***

1. Perhaps the BIGGEST problem is, in my view, the TERMINOLOGY being USED, to DESCRIBE the various FACETS of PEOPLE: that these tend to be based upon the PHILOSOPHICAL CONCEPT of FREE WILL.

2. *Whereas the TERMINOLOGY used in SCIENCE, or thus, OBJECTS – and even for MONEY – and MONEY-MAKING – are based upon the philosophical concept of DETERMINISM.*

***

And the OTHER big factor: unlike PEOPLE, and LIFE-FORMS, in general, OB-JECTS do not employ DECEPTIONS.

So, the FUNCTIONING of a CAR, say, or a project that will become a COLONY on MARS, say, is not DUPLICITIOUS, as part of its makeup.

And this element of DUPLICITY makes UNDERSTANDING, all the more DIF-FICULT.

Chapter 10
So, WHAT IS a GIFT, Compared to Getting a Skill or Self-Improvement Efforts?

P erhaps a GIFT is simply stated as this – at least, for now:

1. "A GIFT is a great ASSET that CANNOT be garnered WITHOUT PAYING a PRICE: a price in PAIN-currency."

Secondly, too:

2. "A GIFT is something we would not even find ourselves being ABLE to logically *ENGAGE* in PURSUING by the pursuing of the MASSIVE PAINS to be INCURRED, because the OUTCOME would be TOO UNCERTAIN, too much of a LONG SHOT."

***

And what is so LONG-SHOT about the PAYOUT of PAIN-LEARNINGS?

It seems, to myself, that MASSIVE pain is very, very frequently TIED to PEOPLE, and then will have the BAGGAGE of BITTERNESS, attached TO it.

__Noting, too, that perhaps in only a slim number of cases, has PAIN taught one much, and yet, without a permanent side-effect of BITTERNESS.__

Chapter 11
What is NECESSARY for us NOT to see pain-lessons through a lens of BITTERNESS?

This is so seemingly trivially-stated, yet so crucial, I would say – again, in my view:

That, as per JOHN MILTON, the poet, in the 1600s, we can say, likely,

"The mind is its own place and in itself, can make a Heaven of Hell, a Hell of Heaven."

***

Or put another way, how we VIEW our Pain – our HELLS on EARTH – how we FRAME it, you might say, is EVERYTHING.

***

And WHAT MAKES for this "MAKING" of what we EXPERIENCE, or thus, of how we FRAME things?

Likely, I would say, OUR WORDS.

***

And thus, our WORDS make our Hells, or our Heavens.

***

Finally, might we note that our so-called LIMITING BELIEFS, or our MINDSET, or our INCORRECT PREMISES, are MADE out of WORDS?

Just like, in a way, LIGHT is made of PHOTONS.

Chapter 12
Our WORDS take our PAIN and make either SWEET LEMONAID or BAD-tasting POISONS

So, at the risk of sounding trivial, I would say it appears to myself, that it is our WORDS that are the CATALYST – or our ACHILLES HEEL, else – in HOW we PROCESS the PAINS in our lives.

And that, then, the REASON WHY it is such a rather UNPREDICTABLE OUT-COME, to GO THROUGH pain – and MASSIVE pain, is PRECISELY because most do NOT KNOW the LEVEL of the QUALITY of the WORDS they HAVE, by which to PROCESS this pain.

And so, we simply say, "PAIN is a LONG-SHOT", because we tend not to have been GIVEN a good TOOL-KIT, when it comes to our WORDS, by which to REFINE this pain, into something MORE than just a LUMP of PAIN-CLAY.

***

So, might we say, NO PAIN = NO GAIN?

But as a corollary, that the GAIN MAY ALSO come with MASSIVE SIDE-EFFECTS, especially, the SIDE-EFFECT of BITTERNESS?

A MIXED BLESSING, thus?

A MIXED SET of GAINS, thus?

***

HENCE, to GET ONLY GAINS, and not GAINS + SIDE-EFFECTS, we need to PROCESS this pain with GOOD, not INFERIOR, *TOOLS*?

The tools of our WORDS, words that enable us to ENCODE what we SEE or READ – in NON-BLAMEFUL, NON-ANGRY fashion – words that SEE PEOPLE as COMPLEX, and subject to CAUSE-and-EFFECT, not WHIMSY?

For EINSTEIN said, "GOD DOES NOT PLAY DICE WITH THE UNIVERSE".

And he might well have been THINKING, too, "GOD DOES NOT PLAY DICE with PEOPLE, as well as not with the INANIMATE parts of the Universe."

Chapter 13
GIFTS vs a TYPE of "SCHOOLING"

So, what makes a GIFT so DIFFERENT, than TRADITIONAL, BRICK-and-MORTAR schooling, or, say, those mentioned earlier, such as The School of Hard Knocks, or The School of Religion, or The School of NO-THINKING?

This is my thinking these days....

That there are TWO TYPES of WAYS to LEARN, basically:

1. The persons who seek to <u>DOWNLOAD</u> the Best Way to Live.

vs.

2. The persons who seek to PUT TOGETHER their own <u>COOKBOOK</u>, as to the Best Way to Live.

(I think this was referred to, in a way, in the movie "No Reservations", when an analyst said to a client, words along the lines of, The best RECIPES are the ones you CREATE, YOURSELF.)

[Rather than the Recipes you DOWNLOAD, I would paraphrase].

But what if we were to EXPAND this, somewhat, and say,

"The BEST LIVES are the LIVES which have the BEST COLLECTION of Recipes INSIDE them – the BEST RECIPE-BOOK", in other words.

Chapter 14
Massive PAIN May Be the ONLY MEANS of QUESTIONING What is Overwhelming to Us

I would tentatively say that we tend to be taught some ideas as "GOSPEL TRUTHS", that are NOT CORRECT.

And that, alas, it strikes me that it tends to take a so-called "ACT of CONGRESS", generally, to CHANGE some of these "views".

Because it appears to be like the LAW of INERTIA:

> *"Law of inertia, postulate, in physics, that, if a body is at rest or moving at a constant speed in a straight line, it will remain at rest or keep moving in a straight line at constant speed unless it is acted upon by a force."*

(The first of Isaac Newton's Laws of Motion.)

Noting, too, that Galileo talked of this:

"Galileo deduced from his experiments that a body in motion would remain in motion unless a force (such as friction), caused it to come to rest."

***

So, what IF our CORE BELIEFS tend to function in the SAME manner as these mentioned "BODIES", only, instead of TANGIBLE bodies of MATTER, thus, we are talking, INSTEAD, of BODIES of KNOWLEDGE – of DATA – that are termed BODIES of BELIEFS – or CORE Beliefs – or PREMISES, in short?

***

And, IF a Core Belief – or PREMISE – is INCORRECT – this too would then "REMAIN IN MOTION", FOR LIFE, unless a "FORCE" caused it to COME to REST?

And WHAT IF the ONLY "FORCE" that were STRONG enough to DO this CAUSING, were MASSIVE PAIN?

And that ELSEWISE, we have what are termed DYSFUNCTIONS, as originating in what we label as "LIMITING BELIEFS"?

***

Some may refer to these as "limiting beliefs", or "lies we tell ourselves", or denials, or "delusions", or logjams, or what have you.

***

And that these can greatly VARY, depending on whether one is raised by someone who reads a lot, or little.

Or whether raised by someone in one country vs another.

Or whether raised by someone of one ethnicity or another.

Or whether raised by someone of one religion, vs another religion.

Or whether raised in an URBAN area, vs a RURAL area, vs what one could term an ISLAND UNTO ITSELF.

Or whether raised by someone who views sexuality in one way, vs another way.

***

This list not being utterly exhaustive....

Chapter 15
To Contact the Author

T he author welcomes any and all comments and suggestions, and would very much enjoy chatting with you....

message@goldpogo.com

Author
Mt Mitchell North Carolina

Author a couple of years' back...

To my parents, who made this possible.

For instance, my mother, an immigrant from eastern Poland, having come to America at
the age of twelve, after a two -week long boat journey, to Ellis Island....

My mother as a young gal in Europe, before coming to America

And to my father, too, a most astute Trainer in life....

Brought up in the ghettos of Philadelphia; left school at the age of seventeen; and later acquiring a GED and going on to obtain a Ph.D. degree at a major University in English Literature; who thus led to my interest and pursuit of writing at a very early age; and too, with respect to his love of photography, which also rubbed off on me.

Hence, "The apple doesn't fall far from the tree"?

Training!

Then, too, my grandparents:

For significantly, my grandmother raised me during my first four years, in my waking hours. And her husband – my grandfather – worked in the tool and die industry for cars; she, born in eastern Poland, like my mother, and was a farmer there; he, born in Odessa, Ukraine, and a Mennonite, and herb-collector and maker of many grandfather clocks in his spare time, on their farm in Michigan:

Grandparents in Niagara Falls

And to my farm experience, as a youth, each summer, in Michigan:

*My great-grandmother, and my mother, and I, when I was seven or
so, on my grandparent's farm*

Then, too, to a man of great impact upon myself, too, from the ages of twelve to fourteen,
starting when I first sought him out to help me obtain a ham radio license at that age of
twelve:

*Mr. Foster; who interestingly did have a foster child he raised
when I knew him; he helped me obtain my ham license; he
hunted; he took me to ham conventions and camped with me; he
collected stamps and coins; and let me build electronic projects
in his workshop; and even took me for a ride on his motorcycle,
popping a wheelie*

And finally, to "Religion":

Again, that of my grandmother, a Baptist; and my grandfather, a Mennonite from
Ukraine - born in the city of Odessa.

*The ethnic Baptist church I attended in the summers,
when a youth, while on the farm the other six days of the
week... German was spoken....*

And to my parents' religious influence upon myself, too: for they almost became mission-
aries in the Plymouth Brethren Church – a group similar to the Amish, Mennonites, and
Quakers: they were to be posted to Canada.
And to L'abri, started by Francis Schaeffer. Where I spent a week in training, at the
Massachusettes branch, in 1982.

And later, other faiths, too....
Including the faith of the Native American Indians, whom I first came into contact with
when living in California, having spent time exploring Arizona; and too, in Cherokee,
North Carolina, and Vonure, Tennessee:

*A photograph I made while visiting the Cherokee Indian
Reservation in 2021, camping nearby for four days in a
tent, in the Blue Ridge Mountains*

*I made a visit to Vonure,
Tennessee, in 2021, to learn
more about the Chero-
kee Indians. Amongst
the sights was the Se-
quoya Birthplace Muse-
um, featuring Sequoya, who
had single-handedly cre-
ated the Cherokee alpha-
bet, under great duress. I
again camped, this time in
the Cherokee National Park
near Vonure, for several days*

Refund policy

REFUND INFORMATION

Desire a refund? No problem: 100% refund, for any reason at all, and absolutely no questions asked, period. And no time limit on this offer. I recognize that sometimes, purchased items are discovered to simply not be a "good fit", or for any number of other reasons....

Loran Joly

If for any reason you desire a refund or desire to leave a comment,

please contact me at:

message@goldpogo.com

or

ReEnvision Press
Box #1036
1303 US 127 South
Suite 104
Frankfort, KY 40601